Raised Underground

Raised Underground

-

poems

-

Renate Wood

Carnegie Mellon University Press
Pittsburgh 1991

Acknowledgments

Grateful acknowledgment is made to the following publications, in which these poems first appeared, sometimes in a slightly different form:

The American Poetry Review: "The Landing," "Before School," "The Button," "Landscape with Cat," "Cabbages," "The Woman Who Wanted No Comfort," "The Suitcase," "First Love," "The Pig," "The Pilot," "Solitaire," "The Mound of Eggs"
The Massachusetts Review: "The Glass House"
The New England Review: "Man and Boy"
Seneca Review: "The Chill"
Prairie Schooner: "The Tree," "Wilderness," "Blood"
Calyx, a Journal of Art and Literature by Women: "Knives," "For M.G."
Warren Wilson Review: "The Man in Front of the Hollywood Wax Museum"

Publication of this book is supported by grants from the National Endowment for the Arts in Washington, D.C., a Federal agency, and from the Pennsylvania Council on the Arts.

The author wishes to thank the Corporation of Yaddo for its support.

Special thanks to Lisel Mueller, Ellen Bryant Voigt, Michael Ryan, Stephen Dobyns, Debra Nystrom, Joy Manesiotis and Janet Holmes for criticism, encouragement and friendship; to Margaretta Gilboy whose painting "Digging for Treasure" gave the impulse for the poem of the same name; and to Bill Wood who helped in too many ways to name.

Library of Congress Card Catalog Number 90-84779
ISBN 0-88748-109-4
ISBN 0-88748-110-8 Pbk.
Copyright © 1991 by Renate Wood
Printed and bound in the United States of America
First Edition

Contents

For Renate and Joachim Hartisch

When I speak to you
about myself, I am
speaking to you about yourself.
How is it you don't see that?

—*Victor Hugo*

Landscape with Cat

Upstream, they say, there are pools between rocks
where the light reaches down to the bottom, and fins
flash beneath you like coins. But here downstream
the river's brown with silt, and the heat creeps
from the muddy banks up to my house. No matter
that I close the shutters to save the few
cool pockets inside whitewashed walls,
dank air penetrates the rooms, my head.

Caught in the eddy at the river bend, the bloated
carcass of a cat spins like a clock hand.
When my stick returns the corpse to the current,
its skin bursts open, flashing fat maggots
that wriggle and sink out of sight.
And part of me floats with the cat downstream
past gardens with garlic and aubergines, past brown men
bagging onions in the small shade of their hats,
through pastures of ruminating cows,
and then through the fields spread with manure
for a late crop. I hear the cries of my family:
uncles, cousins and aunts, my grandmother's
husky voice, the whining of a child, all furious
at being ploughed under
with their habits and few belongings—

back in the eddy, near the surface,
silvery backs blink and are gone.
How I envy them their cold blood,
those pools upstream they will return to
without the slightest trace of memory.

Anniversaries: Berlin

A tank creeps through the rubble of a street.
It could be the street where I was born.
It could be any street reduced to black and white.
A few men scramble hunched under packs and guns.
Now the color comes back on with the groomed newsman,
the evening voice in my living room.
It's been forty years, and outside,
his chest bronzed in the late light, my son
is mowing the lawn, but he can't
drown that ticking in my calendar,
that mine set to go off at its appointed time:
my mind shoots backwards and metal scrap
flies toward my arm to match its jagged scar—
It was spring then, a black and white spring.
The starlings wouldn't stop fixing
their blackened nests, and in shelters underground
the children's pale faces wandered
through rooms that had collapsed on top of them,
still naming the pictures on the walls—
Now when the color fades from the screen,
as though the past were kept on separate reels,
I am an alien here, a girl raised underground,
my sky a sheet of cement, while above on a blue planet
a young man walks barefoot through grass.

(V.E. Day, 1985)

The Arm

When the cast gaped and revealed
that it had healed crooked,
they broke it quickly again, there
before her eyes in the hospital room
between the stretchers of the wounded.
She shot up with her scream,
a stone spat from its sling into a space—
whitewashed and level as the ceiling—
from where she watched
a girl's stick limb crack under fists
and then a hump collapse into a polished bruise.
Pain, she decided then, came
with anything crooked and belonged
to no one in particular,
but was there, plentiful, like air:
indifferent and invisible and necessary.

The Pilot

Face down on the sled,
limbs sagging into the snow,
he was huge—like an old spruce
after it's been felled, no longer
foreshortened by our upward glance.
We hadn't known a man looks bigger
when he's dead. This was not
the enemy we'd seen above us after school
soaring across the valley
no bigger than a pencil sharpener,
this was a man—torn overalls,
a birthmark on his neck.
If only he could see us now from above,
that circle surrounding the sled
like filings neatly arranged
around a magnet's length: kids
staring with squeamish stomachs
smaller than his fist, nuns with flapping gowns,
nervous wings against his stillness,
teenagers with swastikas
on their skinny arms and those old men—
mere dwarfs compared to him.
He lay there so quietly, as though
not to scare us, to keep
the order of the field intact, and yet we knew
that he was frozen there in place, as frozen
as that bloody rose below his mouth in the snow,
while the small puffs of our breath
steamed up and fused, looming
briefly, but larger than he, in the air.

The Hotel

It sat under a hood of snow and pine,
a burrow rich with dens,
and we inside: mothers and children,
nuns and forty-nine orphans, in rows
of rooms like little breathing pockets.
Outside the war roared on, the whole
world at war the women said,
all its countries, all its people.
But we lived in rooms
like boxes stacked row on row.
The lights went on and off, and the corridors
stretched from one end to the other.

In bed next to my sleeping sister
I am alone in our room. My mother
turns off the light and leaves us
after we're tucked in, to sit
with her mother and her sister in a room
at the far end of the corridor
under the lamplight: three women knitting,
shadows in their laps and their words
stretched taut like threads, counting
the loops on the long needles.
Some nights I think they're counting
the rooms of my life. If I were there
under the light, they might show me
rooms like so many lanterns, lit up
and flickering with people and voices,
flickering with all I wish to do.
But they'd never show me
the room I want to know about the most,
the one that waits like a black box
and is still and incomprehensible.

Cabbages

I can no longer talk to cabbages
the way I did when I was ten, but still
each time I cut through cupped leaves
into the heart, I hesitate. When I was ten,
for months, on my way home from school,
I stopped at the glass case of photographs
where a girl dressed in white
lay in an open casket hung with vines.
My mother said it was distasteful,
such pictures of the dead.
My sister's photograph was taken
laughing and waving to us from a sleigh.
After the funeral I buried her doll
in the cabbage bed. I knew my sister was watching
from the rocking chair by her window,
her white-blond hair bobbing
with the motion of the white butterflies
that bounced from cabbage head to cabbage head.

From that day on the cabbages
were my witnesses. At night under the full moon
I could see them from my window,
an assembly of skulls
that had pushed through the ground
for a breath of air. Then I understood:
the dead demand attention, expect to feed
on your loneliness, your games, your rituals.
My sister wanted to hear herself
in my voice, use my hands
to pick the caterpillars from the outer leaves,
and when she tired, sleep
inside the white layers of the heart.

The Cross

(Steiermark, Austria, 1944)

Outside the village, the old cross—
its iron foot propped up with stones—
boosts one more crucifixion
beyond the churchyard and the slate
onion of the steeple.
But it's not that. The chiseled sign
commemorates the place where the Black Death
was halted in 1668, the town saved.
Halted is the word that stops me
swinging my catechism after class.
With a stick I draw a line
extending each blunt arm of the cross
from where its midday shadow marks
the dirt, a line deep enough
to be a trench for ants.
And for a moment I am safe:
squatting on the safe side,
I look across the dusty boundary
past the foot of the cross
to where I now can see the bodies
piled up neatly skull to skull
and shoulder to shoulder
like river rocks jutting out from a wall.
You are alive, they say, *alive.*

The Spark

I can still see him, as I saw him then,
the bearded man, his high forehead,
his body half-wrapped in a cocoon of cloth
and floating on air, his index finger
stretched out to touch the index finger
of another hand, passing—my mother told me—
the spark of life. It was bedtime.
I was sitting on her lap, and the book's
weight pressed on my thighs.
I can still see it, as I saw it then,
the spark traveling down the tube of his finger
like a voice along a wire, see it emerge
from the tip under the roof of his nail
and leap over to the waiting finger
as an answer leaps to a question.
And there it traveled up the length of an arm
and on through the long channels
where it flashed on the glistening walls,
a beam, the pulse of a sentence
that said everything. I can still see
my finger move to the center of the page,
feel the hollow inside my fisted palm
burning from a small fire, as I held it
and wouldn't let go.

Woman Raking Leaves

Some hundred trees in the orchard
have borne their fruit. Now the leaves fall.
Some days empty that way
until there's nothing left but memory.
That's when I think of a woman raking leaves
who wields her rake with a fierce passion,
each stroke meant to gather up her life.
It's not the grass, surfacing like a clean rug,
that she's looking for, nor what is buried underneath,
but the neatness of leaf piles in their predictable rows,
their equal spacing, their measurable height.
Every new mound gives her the fresh strength
of a new lover eager for her embrace.
Caught in the rhythm of her rake
she worships order. Ten mounds to the East,
ten to the West—order, her mother used to say,
is the essence of beauty. When she stoops over the rake now,
leaf piles hide her house; a moment ago
her husband and children waved from the window,
now they're gone—she's lost sight of the steeple,
the whole town. The slight resistance of the leaves
guides her like snags of memory, and when she sinks
her arms up to her shoulders into the rustling piles,
she embraces the whole orchard, once out of reach,
now mapped out neatly on the solid ground.

The Landing

When I first knew you
I thought I had met you before
on a wide flight of stairs
in a Victorian house
where I once lived.
You had my father's
high forehead, and we made love
using my red skirt as a pillow
on the landing between two floors
where the drapery of a high window
stirred like a heavy eyelid.
Under my hands your ribs
were rails guiding me
up and up toward the white door
of my room. Pictures crowded the walls
with bears and bearded giants;
against the mirror on the chest
was the photograph of a small girl
laughing and straining against a dog on a leash,
whose neck was thicker than her waist.
Then when you moved inside me
I knew the dog was unleashed,
his tongue excited, his fur glossy,
his low growl fusing with our voices.
And when you joined the others
in some distant pocket of the house,
a tall woman in a white apron
scolded me about the dog running free.
I sat down on the steps waiting,
not for you, not for him,
but for the little girl, her leash dangling,
breathless, with a rosy face.

The Chill

I.

After the temperature dropped to twenty below,
two finches dipped in the warm water
I had poured into the bird bath
and then froze their wet feet
to the wire fence. There they fluttered
in a desperate dance
until I went outside again
with a kettle of warm water and freed them.

Is that the way you rescued me?

II.

For months, for years, I had dreamed of soldiers
with watches up to their elbows
kicking in doors, of sleeping
in a freight train on a crate,
of the camp with one family per cot.
Each night I ran down the tracks after the freight car
from which my family's tiny figures
waved, while I fell further and further behind.

You caught my frenzied hands
and woke me in your arms.
There was the house with geranium pots,
tea kettles, children like fat puppies—
O Glück, O happy family. I sliced onions
by the kitchen window for our stew,
watching the geraniums burst into bloom,
until I cut my finger: and suddenly
the tea kettle whistled,

it was the train, I saw the geraniums
shaking like bloody lies. Nights while you read,
I sat on the porch watching the mosquitoes
bite my wrist, sparks
in their bellies, trapped alive.

III.

I left when the first snow fell.
Your letters came in their white envelopes,
one snowfall after another. Each day
I put two logs on the fire and watched
their yellow tongues, the hiss and sputter
of the pitch and the grey glove of cinders
slipping over the sparks.

Once when I went out for wood
a big icicle hung like a glass tooth
over my head. For a long time I couldn't move,
transfixed by its glistening weight.
At noon it was almost gone,
but in the drift below the overhang
there was a deep hole where each small drop
had drilled its scar.
Come as far as you can,
your last letter said, *I'll come
and meet you there.* Then I saw you
running down the tracks after the train:
I was standing by the open door, and when I saw
how breathless you were, falling hopelessly behind,
I jumped and landed near you in thick, fresh snow.

The Angel's Fingernail

Some mornings I wake with dread.
I don't love you any more.
Your noisy breathing irks me,
or your words last night limped
through the room like an old man,
and the lines around your mouth are deeper—
overnight some angry angel
ran his sharp nail
across your face. While I wasn't looking
you buried your wit, your beauty,
your spark of recklessness
as my mother buried her silver
under a stone behind the barn
in uncertain times. When, when will they be over?

The Man in the Crane

He was the man with the metal arm
who could lift the most awkward girder beyond the roofs
and smoothly set it down where it belonged.
I had a fear of heights.
He would teach me to love heights,
I would teach him to love the ground.
I staked out my bed on the earth below him,
a rock by my head, weeds by my feet.
He hovered above me, aloof in his cockpit,
his words falling like summer rain.
Now and then he came down for the night.
In the dark I hardly recognized his face,
but I held him, felt the pull of each bone
like a lever under his skin, while my pockets
grew heavy with moisture and roots.
There was a time when I would wait for him
to descend, when I climbed twice a day
up the steep ladder to catch
a glimpse of him working his levers.
Briefly our children lived between us in the trees
like birds and were gone.
We're always waiting for each other:
years made of waiting, months of hesitating.
If I stood on my head could I fall toward him?
Or could he one night in December
dive white and still into my outstretched arms?
Sometimes he waves or his voice drifts down,
a plucked feather. If we wait longer,
could we learn to love the distance
between us like a tuned string?
All winter we'd pick its fine edge
with stiffening fingers and listen.

Letters to China

I.

Today I write to you from a house by the beach,
a house I don't own, not yet,
but last night I dreamt of its white siding,
its windows facing the sea.
There was a sand drift by the door, as if
nobody had entered in a long time.
Inside I found no table, no bed,
but through the window the ocean
churned rough, tossing its beds of kelp.
I watched four men climbing over the rocks
onto the sand, one after the other.
Over their shoulders, like zoo keepers
hauling a giant snake, they balanced
a limp black leg, a tentacle
with suction cups like dead eyes.
Once in another life
we nursed a monster.

II.

Is it still yesterday where you are?
Or am I trailing behind you?
Our letters pass each other in the air.
And when I read your words from Shaoyang,
written at the station with a gloved hand,
you are no longer the same man
miles further south now watching
the red-robed monks at Lianping
as they file into the stone courtyard—
fresh blood, you say, *pulsing through old veins*.
Ours is not young love.
It has raised children and let them go.

It has shaken us, squeezed us,
and sucked our blood. Now I am
discovering its stillness:
cradled on the patched rubber float
I let the waves wash over me
with their oiled palms.

III.

All these years I have been on a train
loaded with old freight: corpses,
some still well preserved,
some not recognizable any more.
I took them from city to city,
I fanned away the flies and stopped
to purchase ice to keep them longer.
And back we went to Breslau, Riga, to Berlin.
Childhood is a cargo we clutch
closer than love. See that boy
at the station with his small bag?
You will give him a free lift on your train.
You will buy him candy or pop.
You will bed him down with a blanket
for the night. *Don't worry,*
you will tell him, and forget me.
And I do the same, when the girl
gets on with her stuffed doll.
I tell her stories. I point out
the Rhine to her, the Mosel. I follow
all her commands, soothe her instead of you.

By now you must have crossed the reed bridge
over the river you still can't spell.
I sweep the sand from the porch and watch,
over one shoulder, rails in the distance,
steam rising, a coiled tentacle, fading and gone.

IV.

Your letters come with the gulls
and the shells I pick from the sand.
And today walking home
with the wind pressing against my back
I found the memory of your hands,
as if it had been sleeping inside my skin
and now was waking and stirring.

The Button

My grandmother lifted a button out of her purse.
"This is the future," she said—
hiding her face in her arms
on the table my mother had built from scrap
at a time after the war when you couldn't buy anything.
In my memory that moment is a whitewashed room
where I sit by my mother's table
sewing the button onto the seam of my shirt.
It's the first button I've ever sewn myself,
and my needle moves awkwardly
in and out of the four narrow button holes.
Every time I wait for the needle's silver point
to appear like a dangerous star, I think:
"This is the future." And suddenly I know
that being afraid of the future
is being afraid of a thought—
the thought of that needle pricking my finger
the next time it comes out of its pit;
the thought that my missing father
will not return. The thread makes a white cross
between the button holes, a cross that fattens
like a chalk mark in school when we do additions.
The future is an addition, a balloon tied to the wrist,
and without me sitting here thinking,
it wouldn't even exist. Severing the thread with my teeth
I resolve never to forget this button:
whatever happens to me from now on
will be connected to this moment,
button after button down the front of my shirt.

The Tree

(Astrakhan, 1895)

Each May the boys pulled the old dory
from the shed. She and her sisters,
already in crisp summer skirts, scrubbed
the benches, placed the oars' iron rings
over their pegs, and off they pushed
onto the flooded steppe. The first strokes
moaning till all the winter rust rubbed off,
they circled aimlessly between the tamarisks,
pink blossom veils above the waist-deep water.
But then the boys would steer the boat
toward one of the few cottonwoods.
Ten yards away the tree came suddenly alive:
small rodents quivering on the branches
close to the trunk, further out birds and insects
rising, filling the air with a hum. Then,
when the boat drifted beneath the outer branches,
she saw them, thicker than a grown man's thumb,
their stiffened bodies stretched out toward her,
forked tongues splitting the air above her head.
And ducking against her cousin's chest,
she heard herself scream, his sweaty hand
stroking her knee that wasn't hers,
that could have been a branch, smooth bark,
not part of her, but of that tree.

The Mound of Eggs

From a great distance
your voice tells me over a pale white phone
how much you miss me, how you can't wait
for me to come home.
I can see you in the kitchen
clasping the fragile shell of the receiver
as if it were holding *us*, as if
what held us for years
suddenly could break. And if it did,
wouldn't we find something inside?
Each fall my grandmother and her Russian cook
rubbed two thousand eggs with lard
and stored them in the basement
inside a mound of sawdust.
Two thousand sealed chambers, cells intact—
I used to think they would last
a life. But sent to fill a basket
I had to reach deeper and deeper
into the mound for the furry shells,
hand and arm tunneling
toward the rough slipperiness of grease.
And when an egg broke in my hand,
I would strip it and let the egg white
ooze through my fingers
until I held only the yolk in my palm
like a moist moon.

Before the Procession

(On the Rhine, 1950)

A slow caterpillar, it crept all morning
through the streets from altar to altar
laid out on doorsteps and sills:

cheap throw-rugs, candles,
a gold-framed saint, or the cross,
smothered in roses or chrysanthemums.

Before they turned the corner by our house,
announced by gusts of Ave Maria's,
I ran down the block inspecting the saints,

their wounds and their skeletal frames,
but it was only Sebastian
who was flesh burst into wounds

like a flowering bush, the crab apples
in the front gardens, as if the arrows
stuck in his chest and limbs

were paint brushes dipped in juice.
How could blood be so brilliant,
suffering so adored? *If it's half as bad,*

my grandmother said, when I cried
for his pain, those points lodged in the bone,
it's only half as beautiful.

Nothing in his suffering gave in to death:
his curls still fluffed over half-open eyes,
his lips still full enough to kiss,

blackbirds feeding in the tree
to which he was tied, plums swelling,
the sun dishing out ray after ray.

Nothing diminished what he was giving up.

The Eyes of the Potato

Weighing each earth-brown tuber in her hand,
my grandmother slid the blade with a circular motion
into the top where it peaked like a scalp,
each revolution baring raw glistening flesh, white
against the dull brown edge marking the blade's path
where the skin unwound, a bandage,
looped from staying so long in place.
Then the clean white body eased from its last wrap,
a tender thing she was the first to touch:
all the lies I ever told my mother
exposed before us, luminous in the late light.
And for a moment I held my breath—those small
black eyes which still remained embedded
in their pocks might see, erupt
to scar what had grown sound and plump—
but then her knife came down
and scooped them from their sockets.

Disruption

Waiting for our children to retrieve
their ball from under the park bench,
we watched a miniature pinscher
racing around the lilac in a frenzy.
And then we stood stunned by the high-pitched whine
piercing the afternoon with its groomed greens,
the teeter-totter, the swings: the pinscher mounted
by a large terrier, both staggering backwards,
after the first arousal now unable to pull apart,
each jerk a spasm of panic and pain.
Fused together—as we, mothers and children,
were fused by the sight of suffering and sex—
they formed a monster, eight-legged, two-headed,
clumsy and comical, and yet this shrieking whine
was almost human, almost the terror of a child.
No sound came from our children
who stared transfixed as if snatched from us.
And suddenly we choked from rage
at this freak coupling that mocked
all the perfections of love we had taught.
When the whine finally stopped
and the dogs trotted off in different directions,
the children quickly resumed their shouts for the ball,
yet we all moved with more caution,
still half-way listening for a new tremor of air or earth,
time bombs ticking under the tidy lawns.

The Pig

When he had hauled it across the cabin floor
my grandfather sat down with his back toward it
to avoid the sight of blood. At the throat,
where the peasant had bled it,
an oozing cut the size of a man's mouth.
It was 1918, in exile, at the foot of the Urals;
they had left a house in Astrakhan
with four servants and a cook. My grandfather
told my grandmother to get her sharpest knife.
Honing the blade on the underside of a pot,
she moved it like a cello bow, her knuckles
white as pearls against the black blouse.
And while their children slept in the furs
on the bunk, and the moon, a poisonous berry,
hung in the window, she knelt and cleft the throat,
slit down across the belly between the rows of nipples
until it opened like a halved fruit.
She remembered later that it took all night,
his voice lifting flesh from bone,
guiding her knife deeper and deeper,
exploring a bottomless wound: all his helplessness
laid out before them on the white cloth
with the chunks of pink loin,
the pale pouch of the bladder,
the bloody, tight-fisted heart.

Wilderness

She had the high cheekbones of a native.
Her mother, expelled from the tribe in Nebraska
when she married a Jew, had later,
after his sudden death, slashed her throat.
Over bowls of stew in the restaurant,
quoting Kierkegaard on madness
she was the well-read campus intellectual.
But after two glasses of wine:
tossing black hair behind her like her story,
playful, with the sure motions of a puma,
her teeth exposed, she growled and hissed
from the pit inside her throat.
She wanted sounds that could carry her
beyond this table and people staring,
slashing through words and definitions
so nothing she knew could hold her back.
And if, right then, she'd turned
and sunk her teeth into my bare arm on the table,
I would have let her. Not because
I was small game, timid and tame behind my skin,
but because I wanted to become
part of what she was then. In such wilderness
you can't tell the difference between joy and grief,
and what lunges from the thickets to hurt
could be what lifts you up.

Digging For Treasure

1. The Chest

My grandmother bent over the chest's dim opening.
Between layers of linens, embroidered handkerchiefs,
thin underwear, her small surprises lay hidden:
a chestnut polished and carved into a puppet's head,
a locket, an ivory comb. She almost
disappeared into the chest, and as I waited
I was afraid that suddenly the heavy lid
might close with a gulp, she would be gone
behind the painted flowers and leaves. But then
she re-emerged, braced against the edge
and out of breath, clasping a portrait of herself—
long black braids, poppies in her skirt—as if
she'd resurrected two women who were one.

2. Knives

After my father was lost in the war,
my mother kept her knives in a box by the workbench
and carved linen chests for the local farmers,
receiving eggs and flour in return.
I would watch her draw the patterns of vines
on the loose front panels, then
with her coarsest knife and a wooden hammer
uncover the outlines of the foliage,
the spirals of the climbers. But I liked it best
when she reached for the finer knives,
carved veins into the leaves and lifted their edges
into curls and folds. "Will you ever marry again?"
I asked, as she was sanding the plump stem
of an ivy leaf. "There's nobody like your father,"
she said and fit the panels to their places.
By the time she was brushing dark stain into the wood,
the lid was closed to keep the inside clean.
Before my eyes the leaves turned brown, and she kept brushing
until her apron under its powdery dust

stood out, a snowdrift in the room.
So I watched her carve chest after chest,
but that morning when I turned seven I found
a small chest by my bed, still pungent with fresh stain.
I lifted the lid, and in my new red dress
my grandmother had sewn, climbed inside
and closed it over my head. There I saw
for whom she made those chests, coffins,
empty as the far side of her bed.

3. For M.G.

"I've buried my sex," you said
after your divorce; after surgery
removed the tumor inside you, that grey rock.
Back in the studio, painting, you can't decide
whether the woman in white, sketched in the background,
kneels by a coffin filled with rocks
or reaches inside a chest for fresh linens.
Her skirt is sealed around her thighs,
a squash blossom closed for the night.
But here in the foreground a woman in red
straightens her sleeves by the mirror,
her skirt swings open around her legs.
Between the women the chest's brown edge
extends, a rhythm of carved notches
catching the light, as though you painted time,
the lapse of months or years between them.
Now it is clear: the two are really one,
and the red dress she's trying on was saved
inside the chest with that red satin bag
now dangling from her belt. Pink lining
peeks through the open slit, each fold glowing
in a deeper shade: the full purse of your sex
unearthed again with all its glittering coins intact.

The Model

(After Caravaggio, *directed by Derek Jarman)*

He bites down
and his teeth hit gold:
coins from the painter
who wants him to hold still,
stripped and oiled to his loins,
flexing his boxer's arms and chest.
The last coin is bigger
and offered from the painter's teeth:
he has no choice but to seize it
with his own—a kiss almost,
as he sucks the metal against his gums.
It's warm as the blade
he carries in his boot.

And so are they all, these models,
bribed by greed and passion
to hold still. In his sleeve
the painter hides his own knife,
while his brush dissolves
each body into light,
that clear and muted fabric
of skin and more skin,
hair and costumes,
satin, fur and pearls—all
held there on the canvas as if
for once they belonged to no one,
as if beauty were stillness
you can neither steal nor possess.
And the painter knows,
off the canvas nothing is safe:
light and love change
like property you can't protect,
like his own scoundrel's life.

Tonight, after the movie,
I stand by the bathroom mirror.
A face looks out

as from a canvas: her eyes
see something I can't see.
And for a moment I want to melt
into her face, as if I could
migrate through glass cell by cell,
enter her iris and skin and there
hold still forever.

The Glass House

After the truck hit the streetcar
I sat dazed in a pile of glass
that filled my pockets and clung
to the sleeves and collar of my corduroy coat.
I remember—after the initial shock—
the glee with which I stood up and walked home
carefully, so as not to disturb the small, jagged shards
covering me like frost. I wanted my mother
to see the danger I had been in, I wanted
to scare her and to tell her I was safe.
"I'm so glad you didn't hurt your eyes,"
she said stroking her hand across my face.

For months I kept the shards in a dish by my bed,
a token of when I lived alone in a glass house
into which my mother peered whenever she wished.
She could see my dolls, my books, my moods, my body.
Her eyes passed by the glass
with the frequency of sun and moon.
There was no place to hide anything,
except what I could gobble down
or stuff into the closet. I swallowed
the longing for my father's lap
where my sister played with his silver watch.
I hid my sister's comb with my cut-off braids
and an unopened package of my father's razor blades.

But the night I watched my mother
sob for my father lost in the war,
I dreamed of standing in a rain of glass,
hard drops hitting the ground, yet leaving me
unharmed. They piled around me,
solid fragments of salt, breath, and grief,
and the next morning, when I opened the closet,
I found my father's watch
ticking under its small hood of glass.

The Woman Who Wanted No Comfort

As a child I knew how to cry my heart out:
nothing could replace that blue ball
my cousins busted with the BB-gun.
No other blue ball would do;
nothing would ever be the same.
And for a while I let the world come to an end,
holding my breath, as if I were diving
straight to the bottom of a lake.
When I surfaced
I had measured the whole expanse of my grief
and owned it, as I had never owned that blue ball—
completely, the way I owned my dreams.
And now? With what stubbornness
I let myself be comforted,
let reason and compromise diminish pain:
when an old lover writes he's marrying,
I lean into my husband's arm;
when my friend died young, I touched her pots
warm from the kiln, told myself she lived;
and when the experts say
there is no hope for this planet,
I go outside and water my vegetables.
Yet last night I woke to a woman's crying,
I listened, stockstill. Her sobbing,
steady as rain, beat on my comforts.
Since then I've thought of nothing but her—
walking all night through unlit streets
she passes strangers and crosses a bridge,
behind her the town's lights on the river
lashed by rain. And there,
beyond comfort, beyond habit and fear,
she opens up her pockets, this woman
who guards her losses like black seeds.

Country Of Amber

1. My Father's Hunting Coat

When he didn't return after the war,
my mother put his coat on my cot
inside out, rolled up as a backrest,
hiding the sleeves, the collar, the deep pockets.
Running my fingers through its thick
brown and white fur lining,
I played with a bear. And once
I pushed the coat's back until it arched
into a tunnel the size of a man's ribcage,
crawled into the hairy skin where it curved
with the bulging of muscles.
Soft tufts brushed my spine and the rough
loden pockets rubbed against my sides.

In the one on the right I found
the matchbox filled with translucent amber chips
we had gathered on a beach.
And I wished for his arms to lift me
to a country where the women wear their amber
polished around their necks and the men return
with the boar hanging by its feet.
But in the left pocket I could feel the lump
of an empty cartridge. Through the cloth
I pressed it against the spot between my eyes
where I remembered his goodnight kiss
and pushed until it hurt.

2. Silver Hands

At their wedding
her husband gave her a pair of silver hands
to fit the stumps her father left her
so she could love no other man.
Her silver hands were long and slender,
with intricate joints—

she could peel an apple
over the sink, comb her long hair,
offer her nipples to her child.
When she clapped her hands they rang like bells:
her friends came running, her husband looked up
from his work. At night the moon played in her palms,
a silver liquid from which he drank
until he fell asleep. But when she stroked him
her hands stayed cold and she felt nothing:
he might as well have been a corpse.
And so she tossed them far into the pond.
That night her husband cried, "What have you done,"
and would not speak to her. And as the hours passed
their silence rose up to her throat, cool water
slapped her face, swallowed her breath,
her eyes. She thought that she would drown,
until she suddenly was lifted up: her stumps
pulling her ashore, stroking the surface,
stroking the silence of her husband's sleep.
And as in the first light she walked down to the pond,
she saw herself on its silver surface
clear and powerful,
and watched the lilies opening,
white hands unfurling, finger after finger.

3. Burial

The first time, the woman who found you sprawled
in the trench that ran through her nursery
buried you among her tulips and geraniums
next to a shattered greenhouse. When I thought of you
there among the pottery shards and scraps of wire
once used for tying bouquets, I saw you
asleep with a tulip behind your ear, your uniform
puffed up into a makeshift bed. The second time,
they moved you to a place where they buried soldiers.
Although they'd given you a box,

I feared they might have left something behind,
a small bone, a button trapped in roots. By then
I was older, and knew your photograph by heart,
my mother's stories of your wit, your love for animals:
a tall man out for the day in the woods,
crossing a stream, a big black dog at his heels.
Now we've brought you home.
The family gathers with flowers, wreaths and hymns.
But when the man in black pulling the dingy cart
arrives at the gravesite, I can't believe
it is you in that head-sized metal urn
with your name and dates scratched in the round lid.
You are so small. Nothing is left:
not the man hunting with a dog at his heels,
not the red flower behind his ear,
not the bullet lodged in his head,
not the hole framed in clean white bone.

Two Countries

The old riverbed behind the house
is a garden of stones and grass.
For years I have worked the soil
and tossed the rocks beyond the wooden ties,
seeded Kentucky Blue within the squared-off plot.
But stones work themselves through the sod,
surface like bullets in an old battlefield.
Each spring I toss them to their hard brothers,
packed in their trenches helmet to helmet,
fist to fist; nights they push
their grey chins between the tufts
which bend over them,
a screen, a green camouflage.
Stone country and grass country—
I step from one to the other
as if I own two worlds:
one ignores the seasons, its veins
older than memory, stubborn as nails
in the rotting fence my family built
at the far end of the lot; one moves
with the seasons, withers, sprouts, then
lifts its green collars into the wind.
In a dream I see fins crossing the lawn,
white under the moon, gills pumping,
and I fear the old bed is running again,
could rise any moment and sweep
away soil, grass, and house.
Next morning nothing but stones
on the grass, fresh growth matted.
And I let it happen again and again:
all the stems spreading like a plush rug
to invite the invasion, the syntax
of stones in the lush language of grass.

Before School

My son spoons the thin milk with his oats so slowly:
he is replacing the words in his mouth
one by one with grey-white flakes, sucking
language back into himself, never to speak to us again.
He is fourteen. These mornings in the shower
he is half-boy, half-man. At table he watches us
from under the pulled shades of his hair.
Bent over coffee cups we look so small and old.
The dullness in our eyes tells him
we dread aging. And when we skim the headlines
our shoulders sag even more, the toast
crumbles in our hands. Yet we sweeten
our cups, slip into our gestures of cheerfulness,
those tired jokes of rise and shine.
How hard we try, how painful it is
to watch us trying, how he despises us for it.
He knows we wait anxiously to hear him talk,
expect some cheery news before he takes off.
Sometimes he thinks we long to hear in him
the future which he believed we'd saved
unspoiled in some hidden place. He hates
these family meals down in the stuffy kitchen.
He'd rather eat alone, upstairs
where the stars on his walls are young.
They sing and swing their instruments
high up on stage, glossed in light and huge.
They're safe. They can't shrink to ordinariness.
They're great, they don't need coffee
to keep them going, they don't complain about the weather.
Yet wasn't there a time not long ago, when we, too,
were faultless, were heroes? When did we fall?
Why did we change? Who put us here
into this grey-white circle, two fish in winter,
nudging the silent lid of the pond?

The Man In Front of the Hollywood Wax Museum

Later you tell yourself
he is an aging extra hired by the museum
for a commercial bit. But on that morning
strolling down the sunny boulevard, dazed from a night
elapsed over a few stubborn lines, you see him
motionless at first, portly, with a combed mustache
and well past fifty, a replica of some tuxedoed
star in a stance of conversation, the way
people stand at cocktail parties,
glass in one hand, except he doesn't hold a glass
in his white glove, it hangs in the air.
A trembling as from an inner clockwork
shakes him into life, each joint
running along a smooth, invisible track.
Now his chin travels the half-circle across his chest
till his head tilts backward and his eyes
sweep across the sidewalk, empty before him,
the traffic humming indifferently on the boulevard,
the window panes of the upper stories across the street—
gathering them all in: *Come,* the white gloves say,
follow me, and they point toward the door
behind which figures wait as shapely as life.
Each of his movements soars—
lighter, wilder, yet more precise than life—
each turn of the wrist a calibrated curve, a dance, a fiction.
And to do this, no matter
that the traffic roars on and no one stops to watch,
takes so much courage: the only way to keep going
is to act as if everything depends on
how you perfect your illusion, as if this
full and lonely attention
is all you have, *is* your life.

After the Movie

In the driveway I flick the headlights off,
and suddenly the snow falls like black lace
before the porch and the lit windows:
I see the table with glasses, the spines
of books against the wall, the slender
body of a violin. Upstairs,
moving from room to room the children's
voices resound, their slippers pounding on the stairs,
while on the kitchen counter the cat
stalks lazily looking for scraps.
From where I watch, all this is the image
of a screen suspended in the night and grained
with tiny icy flakes, not so different
from the Vienna I've just seen, the waltzing
couples flitting by, the chandeliers,
the liveries' silver buttons,
Vienna, the summer of 1914: all would be over soon.
And hesitating in the dark I am a witness,
the cold eye of a camera against the window
where, for a moment, all seems already lost—
so beyond saving: the last black gust
blew out the lights, already carried
the voices past memory and mourning—
nothing is left but this inhuman ashen sky.

Refusal

It wasn't the noise outside—
bombs hitting the bridge and now the station,
the thin man next to her kept guessing targets
as if he were solving riddles: each sound,
shapeless and unimaginable, paired with a once solid thing
to calm her or himself in this hospital basement—

It wasn't the walls squirming as if something
twisted had entered them and the pipes on the ceiling,
which gurgled their senseless alarm; not even
the girl her age slumped over a bucket,
who wouldn't stop spitting blood; not the drain
in her own throat still dumb from the anaesthesia,
the crowd in gauze or splints around her, blurred
shapes, muttering and melting into the dark, no—

It was the long table in their center laid out in white,
festive almost and covered from end to end
with newborns, two rows of white unbaked loaves,
and the few candles in the room flickering
over their faces like tiny white wafers,
eyes and mouths closed—she could barely believe
they were breathing—
                           it was their stillness
that froze her, waiting for one to cry,
to open its mouth and scream
for her and for all. Not a sound from them.

First Love

In 1944 he was seventeen,
the second oldest of fifty Croatian orphans
stranded with us in a defunct hotel
high in the Austrian Alps.
I was six then, with blond braids
dangling over my hips
which weren't yet hips.
I didn't speak his language,
he hardly knew mine.
He was sullen and withdrawn
and only looked up
to watch the fighter planes
when they dipped down into the valley
in the early afternoons. Once
he let me help him
carry the basket for nettles
my mother and the nuns who cooked
made us gather for spinach.
Because he forgot his gloves
he let me pick his share
with my sweaty, protected hands,
and I wished for fields and fields.
Then I dreamed of him
multiplied like the tall spruces
surrounding the hotel,
a whole forest of dreams.
In every one I had wings,
lacy like my mother's gown,
that lifted me up to his height
and above, where I performed for him
acrobatics in the air, stuntflights
plunging from the highest branches
to his feet without ever
touching ground—not kissing him, not
slipping my hand into his, but held there
suspended, an exotic moth
hatched from the black pits of his eyes.

Solitaire

Nights lying next to my husband
I have thought of you as a man
who crosses the bridge to a village
and knocks on the door
of the first house. A woman answers.
You gesture, pointing behind you:
you have traveled for years
to come to this house, this door.
She opens wider and lets you in,
pours beer into your cup, slices
meat and bread. Soon the flow
of questions and answers moves faster,
water rushing over steep terrain,
until it doesn't matter any more
what is said. Your tongue moves
inside the white shell of her ear,
and snow begins to cover the footprints
by the doorstep, blows against the window,
makes the hut a white cocoon.
And I lie here with my ear against my husband's arm,
turning you like a purse in my head, wondering
if this is where I will let you go.

Woman Waving

Over the wing by the window he sits
already proofreading his talk, while she keeps
waving from a berm in the parking lot.
The morning breeze combs through her hand
and blows dust against the pane
with its sealed rounded corners.
He doesn't look up. He thinks she is already
driving back to the house, cushioned in vinyl,
distracted by the voices on the news—
he might as well be a white carp
feeding inside his tank, and she
the shadow of a passing cloud.
But as he turns the page he suddenly sees
a woman walking the snowy field
beyond the printed grid. He knows her
by the color of her hair. She doesn't
wave to him, but wanders through tall aspen,
a blond thread weaving between white trunks,
and all around her, his words, suspended,
are trembling and waving, flocked in the silver air.

Man and Boy

When at the picnic in the movie's last scene
the man sitting on the grass
and the boy he had been at twelve
who had suddenly come running from behind a tree—
when they hugged,
you caught your breath next to me
and released it haltingly
since it had shattered inside your lungs and now
had to be wrenched out piece by piece.
I didn't move, afraid the slightest gesture
would distract you from finding your way
into your own story where you were still a stranger
to yourself. I didn't know whether the boy in you
was mourning for the man, or the man for the boy,
or both; all I could do was wait,
while the people around us shuffled down the aisles,
groping for car keys, mumbling, buttoning their coats.
But you were listening
so intently inside yourself, I kept
looking down the rows of empty seats
for the small figure of a boy
with close-cropped hair, hunched over in his seat,
scarf and gloves still on his lap,
the story not yet over.

The Suitcase

While it was still new
you had left it out on the redwood table in the rain,
perhaps to test its strength,
its sturdy black leather walls, its metal rim,
the plastic label framing your name.
That night, while it was drying
in the summer breeze, its cover open,
we danced around it on the wet lawn,
naked, our skin smooth as birch bark—
while your parents, both old and ill,
slept at the far end of the house,
death's foul taste in their mouths
neither could spit out nor swallow—
danced to a music in your head
I couldn't hear, but could follow in your arms
which held me so gently I might have been the one
in need of all the comfort you could spare.
Later in bed the night closed its black lid,
and we were carried off by a rumbling train,
a cargo dumb with drowsiness,
passing station after station
where crowds with hollow faces stood by the gates,
all clutching the same blank tickets.
And once I was sure an old couple
tapped their knuckles against the thin wall
by my ear, asking to be let in. Startled
I sat up in the dark and found you next to me
asleep with your lips half-parted—
had you said something about grief, something I'd missed,
would never hear from you again?
I heard your father coughing, your mother's shuffling feet,
and water draining, noisy blood from veins,
but you wouldn't wake. Next morning,
you turned the numbers of the silver lock,
so no one but you could open it again,
and we drove to the airport silently, away
from those drawn shades, those half-empty cupboards—
your grief traveling with you from town to town.

The Old Couple

I saw them just for a moment
from the car window this morning
at the intersection of Broadway and Pine,
where there is no stoplight,
and the traffic on the boulevard rolls by
like an unending train. And I still
see them now as I sit here,
as if their slow and careful movements
had entered me, making me slow and careful,
my hand inching along the lines on the paper.
It was windy, and little dust devils,
trapped along the curb, rattled a crinkled
paper cup caught in the grid over the drainage.
They were standing at the curbside
with their shopping cart, as if tossed there,
the man bent over, trying with both hands
to hold on to his jacket, which he had
taken off in the late morning sun and hung
over his shoulders, his shirt sleeves folded at the cuff.
Now the one shoulder of his jacket
was flapping, a nervous wing
wanting to lift him away from this traffic,
and as he struggled to hold it back,
he looked like a wounded pigeon unable to take off.
But the woman next to him stood small and erect.
With one hand she held on
to the shopping cart, while the other
caught her husband's sleeve
like a child's arm before crossing the street.
And now I feel it in my own arm, this gesture
that wants to reach out and guide them
through the traffic, past the gas station
and the recycling center to the brick
apartment buildings, where the antennas on the roof
make small trembling crosses in the wind.

For a moment the way they both
held on to each other crossing the street—
the bags in the shopping cart
nestled like parched cocoons—
this holding on seemed all that love is,
as now my holding on to them
while I sit here is a kind of love also.
And shortly, I will turn off the light,
lie down next to my husband
and think of them, as they lie side by side
in their darkened apartment,
glasses and coins on each bedside table,
as if they had paid their fare.
Their eyes will still be open,
though they can't see anything
but the ceiling with its black ocean
and now and then shapes floating toward them:
small, quick ones colored like memory,
and big ones, made of grey mist
deep in the shadows under the surface,
circling slowly and carefully,
as if they had nowhere to go but had already
reached a final place.

The Clearing

After the loggers left, stumps sat,
pale scars, within a ring
of tall snow-covered pine, of what they once
had been. And now, July, you stepped out from the shade,
your tin pail blinking in the midday sun,
to reach into the shrubs between the stumps
cuffed with the sweetest berries, taut
blue, quick warm explosions on your tongue—
with which it entered you, this clearing,
as you had entered it: it dyed your lips and throat,
the pitch-drenched heat stuck to your breath;
rings oozing where the saw had cut
now cut inside you like implanted ribs—
years not yet lived, things not yet lost—
as if you were already remembering
that taste of being young.
And you thought it was for the berries
you had come, lying face up now in the shrubs,
yourself a tiny stump
under a gauze of heat, bee hum and blinding light.
No, it was so you could look
through ruined spaces, long shafts of absences,
light bare of shade, so you could see,
as if for the first time, what had been razed
still swaying over the clearing.
You could see it, its radiant branches,
or was that you swaying beyond yourself?
If only you knew the word now,
one name for berry, stump and clearing,
it would be like a lid pulled down
between pupil and light,
a screen bearing the burning.

Blood

That day they had slaughtered on the farm,
and a woman came up the road toward the house
with a bucket of fresh blood.
It was war time. We couldn't pay for meat,
but blood was cheap. And with each step
it sloshed from side to side below the white
enameled rim, churning a ring of pale pink bubbles.
We measured salt and spices and watched
the red broth simmering. On the wiped kitchen table
we sliced the loaves of bread and dipped
the porous slabs into the broth now cooling
in our midst. Some of the children screamed
and wouldn't touch it with their finger tips
where, when we dipped the bread, the broth
etched dark red scythes under our nails.
The greased sheets filled with soggy slabs,
we baked the bread till it was toasted:
more brown than red, it tasted of spiced broth.
Some of us wouldn't eat because of its color
or smell or because we couldn't forget
the bucket like a deep, round wound.
But those who did ate all, a whole bucket
soaked into bread, now soaking inside us.
And we thought how this morning the blood
had flowed inside the cow, how it flowed
in all the cattle on that farm, in the horses,
the rabbits, the mice, the birds, and in us.
And we, the farm, the town and towns across all borders
became a pool, a lake, a sea of blood,
one big flood, one single pulse beating,
drumming one syllable over and over again,
and we didn't know, though we kept listening,
whether it was life drumming inside us or death.